Atheist Christmas Coloring Book

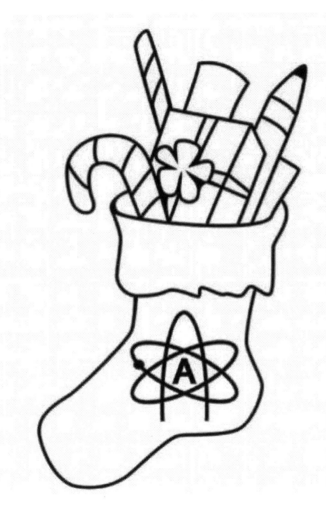

By Rick Marazzani

Illustrated by Claire Viskova

Atheist Christmas Coloring Book   AtheistChristmas.org

It is a custom as old as a custom can be,
Even for atheists like you and me.

Atheist Christmas Coloring Book   AtheistChristmas.org

On the longest, darkest night of the year,
We gather to share joy, gifts, and cheer.

Atheist Christmas Coloring Book   AtheistChristmas.org

No fables or myths are needed to say:
Celebrate peace and love for a day.

Atheist Christmas Coloring Book · AtheistChristmas.org

Christmas is a rich, secular celebration,
built upon wide and diverse inspiration.

Atheist Christmas Coloring Book   AtheistChristmas.org

Baby Jesus was born away in a manger?
Listen closely as things only get stranger.

Atheist Christmas Coloring Book AtheistChristmas.org

Christmas today is a modern invention.
Evolved from prehistoric tribal convention.

Atheist Christmas Coloring Book — AtheistChristmas.org

Some customs date from the Neolithic,
like the horned god Krampus, quite horrific.

Atheist Christmas Coloring Book   AtheistChristmas.org

Winter Solstice is due to Earth's axial tilt,
Mapped by the ancients in temples they built.

Atheist Christmas Coloring Book — AtheistChristmas.org

The Jews deserve credit for lights and leafs.
The Norse the Yule log, Pagans the wreaths.

Atheist Christmas Coloring Book   AtheistChristmas.org

On Roman Saturnalia one did as he pleases.
Then in 300 A.D., the Pope added Jesus.

Atheist Christmas Coloring Book   AtheistChristmas.org

Over 2,000 years, things added and changed.
North Pole, Flying deer, Elves! Very strange!

Atheist Christmas Coloring Book — AtheistChristmas.org

Saint Nick was dragged West in 1087,
to scare kids to sleep by half til eleven.

Atheist Christmas Coloring Book   AtheistChristmas.org

Christmas carols are musical stories,
From oral traditions and allegories.

Atheist Christmas Coloring Book — AtheistChristmas.org

No angels, no demons, no heaven or hell, but if Bigfoot were real he'd think Xmas was swell.

Atheist Christmas Coloring Book — AtheistChristmas.org

Without Jesus or faith then why should we care? Because Christmas is rational when it's stripped bare.

Atheist Christmas Coloring Book AtheistChristmas.org

A season for Love, Joy and Goodwill,
Celebrate them without religion to shill.

Atheist Christmas Coloring Book   AtheistChristmas.org

Feast, share, bond, and be merry,
Christmas is timeless, not prayer-y.

Atheist Christmas Coloring Book   AtheistChristmas.org

Christmas was made via holiday hack,
Enjoy what you like, give the rest back.

Atheist Christmas Coloring Book AtheistChristmas.org

Look past the myths and absurd superstitions,
Start your own atheist Christmas traditions.

Atheist Christmas Coloring Book   AtheistChristmas.org

Wrap up a tree in electric lights, to show how
Science tamed chaos and night.

Atheist Christmas Coloring Book   AtheistChristmas.org

This season is about love and joy for mankind, and enjoying the bounty you've earned with your mind.

Atheist Christmas Coloring Book   **AtheistChristmas.org**

Christmas for Atheists?!?

No one religion or culture has a monopoly on sharing, caring, peace and joy. Before and after the birth of Christ, wintertime "*Christ*mas" traditions existed independently of Christianity. God doesn't control the tilt of the Earth!

Christmas is part of our Western tradition. Over the centuries, local customs were adapted to bring Christmas to everyone, regardless of their faith, or lack of it.

It has always been a special time of year across diverse cultures, and has spread far beyond the West to all corners of the globe. Christmas need not be dedicated to mysticism and supernatural nonsense.

Atheists can embrace Christmas as a mid-winter celebration with friends and family. It is a wonderful time to share family traditions and discuss the rational roots that keep your family strong. No need to eschew Christmas just because of tangential religious connections. We celebrate Thursday without worshipping Thor!

Find out more at AtheistChristmas.org

This book was written by Rick Marazzani, a geek dad, game guy, tech nerd, and objective thinker.

The illustrator is Claire Viskova, a cartoonist and artist who celebrates Christmas with her freethinking family; more of her work can be found clairecartoon.com

Printed in Great Britain
by Amazon